BUCKLES

Alan and Gillian Meredith

SHIRE PUBLICATIONS

M000312910

First published in Great Britain in 2008 by Shire
Publications, Midland House, West Way, Botley, Oxford
OX2 0PH, United Kingdom.
443 Park Avenue South, New York, NY 10016, USA.

Email : shire@shirebooks.co.uk
www.shirebooks.co.uk

© 2008 Alan and Gillian Meredith

All rights reserved. Apart from any fair dealing for the
purpose of private study, research, criticism or review, as
permitted under the Copyright, Designs and Patents Act,
1988, no part of this publication may be reproduced,
stored in a retrieval system, or transmitted in any form or
by any means, electronic, electrical, chemical, mechanical,
optical, photocopying, recording or otherwise, without the
prior written permission of the copyright owner.
Enquiries should be addressed to the Publishers.

Every attempt has been made by the publisher to secure
the appropriate permissions for materials reproduced in
this book. If there has been any oversight we will be happy
to rectify the situation and a written submission should be
made to the Publishers.

A CIP catalogue record for this book is available from the
British Library

ISBN-13: 978 0 7478 0691 2

Alan and Gillian Meredith have asserted their right under
the Copyright, Designs and Patents Act, 1988,
to be identified as the authors of this book.

Designed by Ken Vail Graphic Design, Cambridge, UK,
and typeset in Perpetua and Gill Sans.
Printed in Malta by Gutenberg Press Ltd.

08 09 10 11 12   10 9 8 7 6 5 4 3 2 1

COVER IMAGE
A selection of buckles, clasps, slides and trims from the
nineteenth and twentieth centuries.

TITLE PAGE IMAGE
Enamel clasp. From the late nineteenth/early twentieth
century.

CONTENTS PAGE IMAGE
Clasp. Paint on stamped brass – referred to as 'cold
enamel' (see page 39). From the mid-twentieth century.

DEDICATION
To Katy and Ben, the next generation

ACKNOWLEDGEMENTS
The authors are deeply grateful to Andrew and Vicki,
Angela and Tim for all their help. They also wish to thank,
most sincerely, all the following for their assistance:
Kevin Aitchison, Boys' Brigade, Edinburgh; Janet Targett,
Clarks Shoes; Leila Marvin of Corsets and Crinolines;
Michael J. Cuddeford; Florence Nightingale Museum
Trust; Great Western Trust, Didcot; Sarah Hodgkinson;
Mark and Irene Cornelius, The Holley/Cornelius
Collection, Bletchley Park, MK3 6EB; Anthea Jarvis;
Maureen Needham; Rebecca Shawcross, Northampton
Museum and Art Gallery; The Pump Room, Bath and
North East Somerset Council; Peter Raybould; Fiona
Bourne, Royal College of Nursing Archives; June Swann.

Illustrations are acknowledged as follows: Michael J.
Cuddeford, metal detector finds, pages 5 and 15;
Kevin Aitchison, Boys Brigade, Edinburgh, page 29;
Janet Targett, Clarks Shoes, page 26; The Pump Room,
Bath & North East Somerset Council, page 15.

Shire Publications is supporting the Woodland Trust, the UK's leading woodland conservation charity, by funding the dedication of trees.

CONTENTS

INTRODUCTION

Buckles have a very long history, being indispensable for joining the two ends of straps in a secure but adjustable manner. The importance of their invention cannot be overemphasised but they are usually overlooked and taken for granted. This book aims to give a brief insight into the development and uses of buckles in all their forms. Buckles issued specifically for the military are excluded as other publications cover this subject.

Buckle frames come in many shapes and sizes depending on the intended use and the prevailing fashion. The frame, being the visible part, carries any decoration. It may be slightly rounded to accommodate the curve of a shoe front. A reverse curve indicates that the buckle was intended for use with thick material, the shape making it easier to thread the strap end over the bar. For use with thick leather, the bar was set away from the frame. If the leather was too thick to bend, a plate would be hinged on to the bar and the leather riveted to the plate.

Chapes of various designs could be fitted to the bar to enable one strap end to be temporarily secured before fastening the other. This made buckles easily removable and consequently interchangeable. As buckles were expensive, this could be a great advantage. Unfortunately the teeth or spikes

Metal detector find. Buckle with plate. Medieval period.

Opposite: Various slides. *Left to right. Top* Celluloid, *c.* 1930s. Metal, late twentieth century. Pearl with cut design. *Middle* Black glass discs glued to shaped frame, late nineteenth century. Chrome deco, *c.* 1930s. *Bottom* Moulded plastic, mid-twentieth century. Celluloid, *c.* 1930s.

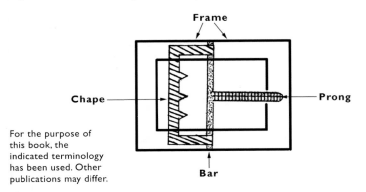

Frame

Chape →

Prong

For the purpose of this book, the indicated terminology has been used. Other publications may differ.

Bar

Above:
Buckle. Blue enamel edged in diamanté, toothed chape. Second half of the nineteenth century.

Buckle. Iridescent pearl with cut patterns. Last half of the nineteenth century.

Right: Utilitarian buckles with various chapes. *Top* 'T' or anchor shape. *Second down* Similar with crossed swords; trademark of Wilkinson Sword. *Middle* Registered number 17803; design registered in 1885. *Fourth down* Marked 'Williams Patent'. *Bottom* Marked 'Pritchard's Patent'. All from the late nineteenth/early twentieth century.

Below:
Buckle. Brass. Bar set back from the frame to take thick material. Steel prong.

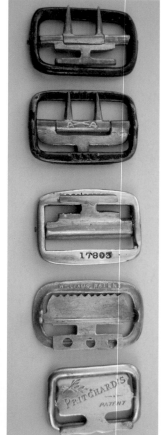

Original card,
c. 1930s.

on the semi-circular chapes damaged the straps or belts, making frequent repairs necessary. Buckles fitted with 'T'-, anchor- or spade-shaped chapes avoided this but needed a slotted end in the belt to accommodate them.

A buckle without chape or prongs is called a buckle trim or a slide. It may have been designed in this way, or it could have lost its prong in use. This type was frequently used in home dress-making, the belt end being secured with a hook and eye, as without any prongs there was no need to do the intricate stitching round the eyelet holes. The same style, as its term indicates, was widely used purely for decoration, particularly on shoe fronts, where it could conceal an unattractive elastic fitting.

The conventional buckle with a frame, bar and prong gives the most reliable and easy-to-use closure for a belt but affords little space for decoration. On the other hand, a solid or fretted plate, with a hook or stout, blunt prong and a chape on the back to take the belt

Buckle. Brass, spade-shaped chape, sharp prongs. Size, 1 inch.

7

Buckle from West Midland Railway bandolier, with reverse showing fittings.

ends, gives plenty of scope for decorative designs. However, a hook in this position may be difficult to do up, and wear on the belt from constant use of the prong in one place can stretch the fabric making it insecure. This style was used on civilian uniform buckles in the nineteenth century and for trouser and jeans buckles in the twentieth century.

Although we casually refer to any device joining belt ends as a buckle, if it consists of two separate pieces, one for a hook and one for a loop, it should be called a clasp. Clasps were particularly popular at the turn of the nineteenth century. Their main disadvantage is that as each belt end is securely fixed to each clasp piece, the size of the belt is not easily adjustable without the aid of an inserted elastic panel.

Great ingenuity was shown by manufacturers in the designs of fully and securely interlocking two-piece buckles. One such type was often used for civilian uniforms as it could incorporate a flat front surface large enough to carry the required insignia. A variation of this type incorporated a removable dagger-shaped spoke joining the two buckle pieces.

Clasps. *Top* Plated metal with rivet decoration, black velvet backing, marked 'Déposé'. *Middle* Tinted brass. *Bottom* Electroplated brass, marked 'Ges Gesch'. All from the late nineteenth/early twentieth century with art nouveau influence.

9

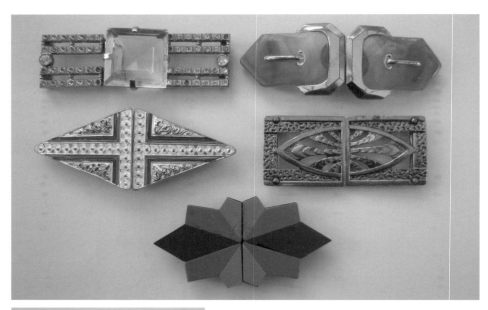

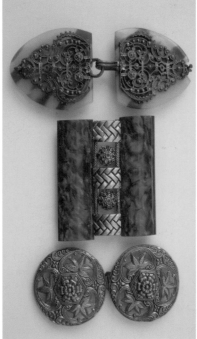

Above: Clasps. *Left to right. Top* Diamanté. Moulded glass with lustre paint. *Middle* Painted metal. Stamped metal marked 'Germany'. *Bottom* Green plastic compound. All *c.* 1930s.

Left: Clasps. *Top* Filigree metal mounted on plastic compound. *Middle* Composition mounted on metal. *Bottom* Pressed metal. All from the first half of the twentieth century.

Below: Clasp. Unusual style of interlocking. Marked 'Déposé'.

Over the years there have been many different types of fixing devices, each invented for a specific purpose and to suit the fashion of the day. For instance, buckles incorporating a movable bar, and relying on the tension of the belt they were adjusting to keep them in place, were discarded as the fashion passed. In the twenty-first century the use of loose-fitting garments is so well established that it is sometimes difficult to imagine exactly how

Belt buckle.
Midland Railway.
Pre-1923.

Advertisement for a
support corset from
a publication of
5 February 1913.

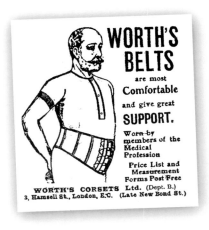

different devices were used and, in some circumstances, the discomfort they caused.

Dating some buckles with definitive accuracy is impossible. Stout brass or white metal buckles for utilitarian use have kept the same design for years. The Records Office at Kew, London, holds data on UK Registered Design Numbers and, if you find a number on a buckle, a little research will reveal the date of the registration and perhaps other information. If the item has a complete silver hallmark, reference to the appropriate books will give the exact date.

A knowledge of fashion can help but styles have been reused, which can be most misleading. Materials also may be replicated. Cut steel for example was used in the eighteenth century, and with different construction in the nineteenth century. The use of paste has been eternally popular.

The setting of stones may give a clue to the date of a piece, but a contemporary jeweller with any skill can produce the cabochons or closed setting favoured by the eighteenth-century artisan.

Selection of buckles
with movable bar.
Top row, middle
Registered
18 March 1949.
Bottom row, middle
Registered 20
January 1949.

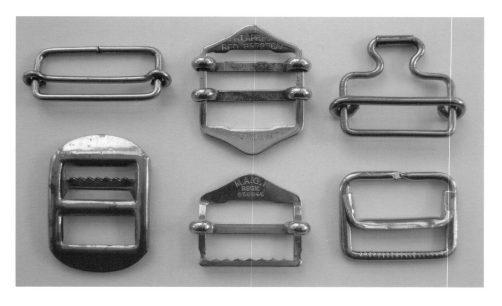

Brass buckle. Inset of green paint, and its reverse showing its Registered Design Number, dating it to 11 February 1909.

Below left:
Clasp and reverse. Ceramic discs mounted in metal. Registered number 388979. The numbers 388979–86 were registered on 22 March 1902 by Norman and Ernest Spittle, 45 Newhall Hill, Birmingham. They were noted as art metal workers.

Below right:
Slide. Hallmarked silver designed to resemble cut steel. Chester 1903. Maker, Charles Horner.

Buckles remained exclusively for the wealthy until, during the fifteenth century, improved manufacturing techniques made a more easily produced moulded item cheap enough to be available to a larger proportion of society.

Once buckles were removed from their original fixing their intended purpose could be forgotten and they were reused in whatever manner was required. Buckles have been used and reused, passing in some circumstances from one generation to the next.

In the eighteenth, nineteenth and early twentieth centuries, buckles were considered most acceptable gifts and many have become treasured family possessions.

BUCKLES TOP TO TOE

HATS

Carte-de-visite of a lady with a buckle in her hat. Late nineteenth/early twentieth century.

BUCKLES have provided an important function in hats. As the pull-on flexible beret style of the fifteenth century was replaced by the larger tall hat with a brim, an exact fit became important so as to secure the hat firmly to the head. This fit was achieved with a band and a buckle. This style was worn by both men and women and became a feature of the Puritan dress of the Commonwealth period in the middle of the seventeenth century.

At the end of the seventeenth century, three-cornered hats, at times flamboyantly adorned with trimmings and feathers, were fashionable, but buckles were still required. Tall hats returned to favour in the eighteenth century, being worn by men and those women who followed a rakish style particularly when out riding. Buckles were still an important feature, bright and gleaming against the popular black beaver-skin.

In the nineteenth and twentieth centuries manufacturing techniques improved. Hats were made of more rigid materials and to exact measurements. These were maintained in wearing and so it became unnecessary to use a buckle to secure the fitting. Any buckles featured were for adornment only.

Hat slide. Thin stamped brass, cut-steel rivet decoration, individually set. Length, 6 inches. Late nineteenth/early twentieth century.

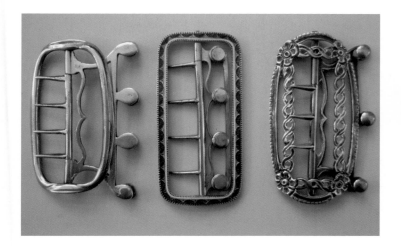

Above: Image taken from a statue in the Pump Room, Bath, of Beau Nash (1674–1761), showing him wearing a buckled stock. *(Copyright Bath and North East Somerset Council)*

Above left: Stock buckles. *Left to right* Plain silver, London *c.* 1758. Blue and white enamelling on gilded brass. Elaborate silver, Birmingham 1790.

STOCKS

During the eighteenth century, gentlemen wore a scarf wound round their necks. Called a stock, it was made of silk, lawn or muslin. Those following the fashion to excess wound the stock from their waistcoat-top to their chin and arranged it with smooth folds in the front. They then used a buckle to keep the stock in place. The buckle had fittings so that the wearer could remove it easily from the stock. The stock could also be secured by tying and is still worn like this in formal horse-riding attire.

CHEST

Some of the earliest buckles known are those used by Roman soldiers to strap their body armour together. These buckles would have been expensive items but purely functional, their strength and durability of vital importance.

Left: Metal detector find. Roman buckle.

Right: Metal detector find. Incised decoration. Of the late fifteenth and into the sixteenth century.

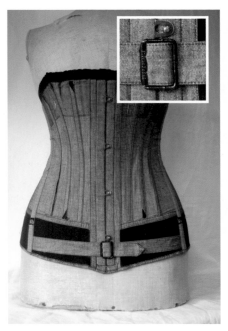

Above: Abdominal corset, c. 1910, used for support and maternity.

Left: 'The New Renown Corset', 1901–10, English. The black buckle is marked 'Unbreakable'.

The baldrick was a belt worn diagonally over the right shoulder down to the waist at the left. It carried the sword, and its buckle therefore was as important as that on a Roman soldier's armour. In England at the time of the Civil War most gentlemen carried a sword, the baldricks being held together by a sturdy plain buckle. After the Civil War, the baldrick remained part of army uniform, while the gentry continued to wear swords as part of formal dress until the middle of the eighteenth century.

Belts of similar style to the baldrick, with sturdy buckles, were used by messenger boys to carry their pouch, and by train guards and bus conductors for carrying tickets and money well into the twentieth century.

Another garment, which today would be likened to body armour, was the Victorian ladies' corset. Although elastic was in use from the first half of the nineteenth century, buckles and clip fastenings were still needed to achieve the restrictive structure necessary for the fashionable hour-glass figure. It was not until the end of the nineteenth century that elasticated material began to replace the use of buckles and clasps. Buckle-fastened corsets continued but for surgical purposes only, where rigid support was vital.

During the nineteenth and twentieth centuries an array of buckles was used on gentlemen's fitted waistcoats. It was important to have a smooth closed front to the waistcoat showing in the jacket opening.

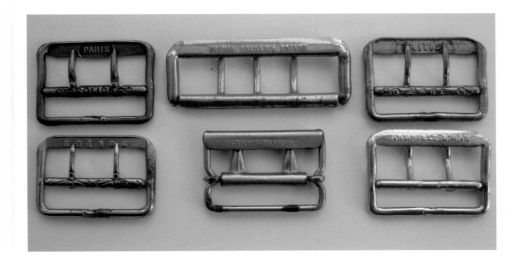

Bespoke waistcoats, made by expert tailors, fitted perfectly, but off-the-peg garments needed fine adjustments. Gussets were fitted down the back panel or at each side seam with straps and pronged buckles for adjusting them. However, the wear caused by the prongs and the inconvenience of fastening a buckle in such awkward positions prompted the invention of many devices. Often these involved winding the loose strap in and out through an adjustable bar. If the garment needed tightening a tug on the strap would pull it into place.

WAIST

Before the sixteenth century clothes did not have pockets, so belts worn at the waist were used by men to carry a variety of items.

A workman's tools were of immense importance to him and where better to keep them than easily to hand tucked into a securely buckled belt? Every working man would carry a knife in this way, perhaps for his own protection, but more often to cut food, as cutlery was not widely available. Pocketed work aprons were introduced in the seventeenth century to carry tools but, if such a garment impeded the workman, he would continue to use a belt, some doing so until the end of the nineteenth century.

Street vendors abounded and all needed to carry their wares and, more importantly, their money pouches about them, from buckled belts.

Ladies, on the other hand, wore loose pockets under their top garments, attached to a band tied round the waist.

In the eighteenth and early nineteenth centuries decorative buckles for the lady's waist formed a relatively small part of the buckle-making industry

Selection of buckles used unseen on garments such as corsets and waistcoats. All have sharp prongs and date to the late nineteenth/early twentieth century. *Left to right. Top* Marked 'Paris' and 'Solide'. Marked 'Thomas Walker's Patent'. Marked 'British' and 'Make'. *Bottom* Marked 'Solide'. The swivelling protector for the tip of the prongs is marked 'Pat Mar.13.1888'. Marked 'Armfield B'ham'.

Interlocking buckles of the sort often used with elastic belting. From the twentieth century.

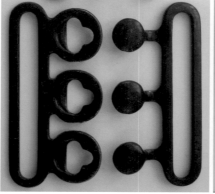

as a whole. However, whenever fashion demanded a distinctive waistline, belts with buckles came into vogue. In the middle of the nineteenth century a belt was used to accentuate the size of the crinoline.

At the end of the nineteenth century a belt and fancy buckle were essential to emphasise the 18-inch waist so fashionable among young ladies. Clothes rationing restricted styles during the Second World War but Dior's post-war New Look, with its long and very full skirt, required a buckled belt to give true emphasis to the style.

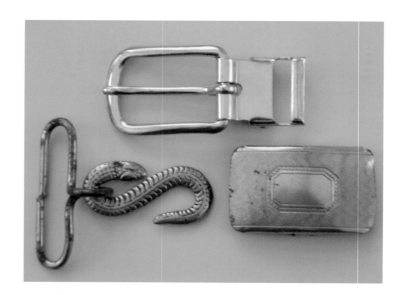

Selection of men's and boys' trouser buckles. From the late nineteenth and twentieth centuries.

Buckles. *Left to right.* *Top* Filigree-work with blue glass mounts, from the early twentieth century. Plastic compound, c. 1930s deco 'D'-frame style. Pressed and painted wood, from the mid-twentieth century. *Bottom* Moulded hallmarked silver, Birmingham 1897. Pearl mounted on silver, Birmingham 1913. Twentieth-century moulded and tinted white metal.

Clasps. *Top* Stamped metal with glass decoration. *Middle, left to right* Watch-cocks converted. Stamped white-metal bow. Filigree. *Bottom* Tinted metal with celluloid inserts. All from the early twentieth century.

Clasp. Tortoiseshell
with gold and
silver inlay. From
the mid-nineteenth
century.

In the twentieth century the demand for utilitarian buckles started to
fade and the fashion industry was the main market. The cheaper ready-to-
wear clothing brought prices within easier reach for women and men. The
introduction of plastics made decorative buckles less of a luxury item, but the
vagaries of fashion still created fluctuations in the demand.

LEGS

In the eighteenth century there was considerable diversity in the style and
function of buckles worn on the leg, from the fashionable gentleman wishing
to emphasise the line of his calf, to the multitude of workmen from the lower
classes who needed protection from the harsh environment of their workplaces.

Throughout the eighteenth century gentlemen's trousers finished at the
knee with a band or cuff that went over the top of the stocking. The upper
classes would fasten this band or cuff with buttons matching those used on
the jacket or with a buckle of quality, such items being important in showing
off wealth and status.

The dress of the working man was somewhat more haphazard, warmth
and comfort being of more importance than display. There were no laws
controlling the use of chemicals, sharp knives or foul water. It was up to the
individual to protect himself, which he did with appropriately shaped pieces
of leather securely buckled over the legs like a cricketing batsman's pad.
These were known, in some areas, as 'spatterdashes'.

In the nineteenth century, refinements in the design of these protective

garments evolved to produce gaiters, which were worn by a broader section of society. The shorter versions of this item, covering the top of the shoe and the ankle and known as 'spats', were worn as protection by some tradesmen such as coal porters and dustmen, as the longer gaiter was too cumbersome. By the twentieth century spats had become a fashion item worn purely for effect by the upper classes.

All these styles generated demand for small strong buckles.

The demand for leg protection of all kinds fell away with the introduction of rubber wellington boots in the 1890s. Originally only the wealthy were able to afford them but by the early twentieth century prices had fallen sufficiently to bring them within reach of the working man.

Trousers finishing just below the knee continued to be worn in the nineteenth and twentieth centuries by the gentleman farmer, by the country sportsman for shooting or by men playing golf. This style of trouser was known as 'plus fours' because of the extra 4 inches of cloth needed below the knee for pleating into the buckled band.

Breeches buckles. *Pair* Brass with 'T' chape, 7/8 inch. *Centre* Diamanté set into white metal, shaped chape. All from the nineteenth century.

Breeches buckle. Cut steel, individually set. Court-dress style.

21

BOOTS AND SHOES

Until the invention of the motor car, horses were the sole means of transport. Spurs therefore were in constant use and by the seventeenth century had become part of everyday dress for men. Strong buckles, slightly butterfly shaped so as to make it easier to insert the leather strap between the frame and the bar, kept spur fittings in place. On shoes for both women and men the use of buckles replaced ties as fastenings from the late seventeenth century.

In the eighteenth century shoe buckles became a focus of fashion. Gentlemen and ladies gave great attention to their purchase, regarding them as they would a piece of jewellery. The buckles were interchangeable and, when not in use, were kept in velvet-lined boxes.

The 'toy trade', the name given at that time to the manufacture of a wide range of small items, was made up of individual specialist workshops. Machinery enabling mass production was in its early stages of development and most small items were still made by hand by skilled craftsmen.

The separate parts of the buckles were made in different workshops. Consequently there was a variety in the design of both the prongs and the chapes. The buckle-maker would buy from whom he chose, frequently using iron parts with more expensive metal frames to keep his product at a competitive price. The frames could be made of silver, pinchbeck, steel or gold-dipped brass or copper, and be set with marcasites or paste.

Fashionable ladies had their indoor shoes made from the same material as their dresses, with flaps each side called 'latchets', one to fit the chape of the buckle, the other to go over the bar. The buckle could be easily removed

Shoe buckles. Hallmarked silver, London 1795. Ferrous-metal bar and spiked chape.

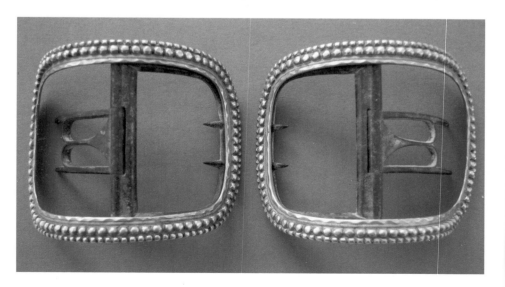

from the latchets although the sharp prongs caused considerable damage to the fabric. Women's outdoor shoes were of leather.

The fashion among gentlemen ranged from discreet oblong brass in the middle of the eighteenth century to exaggeratedly large, flamboyant styles between 1775 and 1795.

In the following years, the effect of the French Revolution seeped through to the fashion world in England and it became unacceptable to be too ostentatious. This brought an end to the fashion for shoe buckles and ties were reintroduced. The change brought about considerable hardship to the

Shoe buckle.
Eighteenth-century.
Diamanté pavé set
in silver, and its
reverse, showing
spiked chape and
'hayfork' prongs.

Shoe buckle.
Eighteenth-century.
Pewter with
copper inlay.

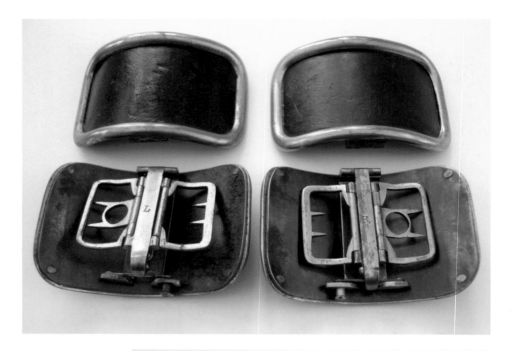

Above: A butler's shoe buckles. Brass rim backed with leather. Reverse shows press-release spring-fitting.

Boxed set of cut-steel shoe buckles for formal court dress. Leather backing. They have the same spring-fastening as the butler's buckles.

Shoe slides. *Left to right. Top* Diamanté. Plated white metal. *Middle* Electroplate, marked 'LW Paris'. Egyptian figures, the design influenced by the excavations of Howard Carter in 1922. *Bottom* Plated white metal. Cut steel individually set. All from the late nineteenth/early twentieth century.

makers and the great number of shops, street stalls and pedlars selling buckles. In response, in an attempt to alleviate the situation, the Prince of Wales, later George IV, an arbiter of fashion, requested that those attending court should continue to wear shoe buckles. Shoe buckles have remained part of formal court dress in Britain.

Through the nineteenth century shoe fastenings for day wear for men remained discreet laces. Buckles were occasionally worn in the evening on fine-leather slipper-shoes. Buckled shoes were part of the livery worn by uniformed company staff and household servants. This type of buckle was made up of a plain or sparsely decorated frame of brass or cut steel, often with a spring fitting.

Selection of twentieth-century shoe and sandal buckles. Those with diamanté (*top row, middle*) could be used on ladies' barstrap-fastened shoes.

In the twentieth century the First World War caused a great reduction in the numbers of household servants. The few remaining continued to wear complete livery uniform with buckled shoes, but only on very special occasions.

Although laces were generally used on walking shoes for both women and men, on ladies' court-shaped dress-shoes fancy buckles or trims were used throughout the nineteenth century and into the twentieth. A development of the court-shoe with a strap across the front at near ankle level created a much more secure fitting. These straps were fastened with either buttons or buckles. Alternatively, to acheive a decorative appearance, a hook the width of the strap was fitted to the shoe. A fancy

Advertisement for the Clarks sandal 'Joyance', produced from 1933 to 1972. (*Courtesy of Clarks*)

CLARKS SANDALS

trim, slipped on to the strap, acted as an anchor when the strap was fitted through the hook, completely concealing it.

At the end of the nineteenth century there was a move among both men and women towards a more healthy lifestyle. Sports such as tennis, and also cycling and walking, became popular. Apart from the laced plimsoll, there was no really suitable footwear available. Sandals were introduced in the early years of the twentieth century to remedy this.

In the UK the firm Clarks produced various styles from 1914 with strong, solid, flat, white, metal buckles. In 1933 they made a version for children. This had a crêpe rubber sole and a stitched-on leather top with decorative holes cut in a daisy pattern. Named 'Joyance', this style was first retailed at 4s. 9d (24p in today's money) and continued in production until 1972.

The buckles on these and other sandals varied through the years but were very plain, white metal, some with offset bars, some with rollers over half of the frame, both devices being designed to ease fastening. Although sandals continue to be worn by some people and in some countries, track shoes, fastened with laces or Velcro, have largely supplanted their use in the West.

Advertisement for Lotus court-shoes from a publication of 5 April 1911. The prices range from 13s. 9d (69p) to 17s. 9d (89p).

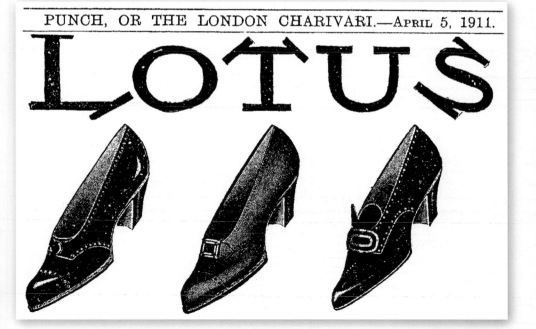

PUNCH, OR THE LONDON CHARIVARI.—APRIL 5, 1911.

LOTUS

OTHER USES OF BUCKLES

CIVILIAN UNIFORM BUCKLES

Nurses' clasps. *Left to right. Top* Hand-engraved EPNS. Moulded EPNS. Engraved silver, Birmingham 1899. *Bottom* Moulded silver, Birmingham 1898. Engraved silver, Birmingham 1907. Engraved silver, Birmingham 1902.

BEFORE the multiple twentieth-century rules on health and safety, civilian uniforms were for display rather than the protection of the individual. Smartly dressed workers inspired confidence and added prestige to the company they represented. Uniforms provoke a unifying bond, helping to build up team spirit while enabling easy recognition of the levels of authority within the group.

During the Victorian period the newly created railway companies in Britain vied with each other in all aspects of their appearance, including uniforms. Each town had its own police force and, although all used the familiar dark blue for their uniforms, each had its own insignia for identification and for generating local pride. Youth groups, such as the Scouts,

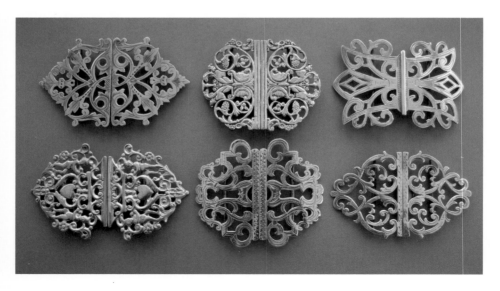

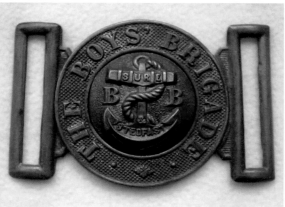

had military-style uniforms. In all these instances, belts and buckles formed an important part, being in many cases used to carry equipment as well as augment the appearance. Firemen, for example, carried their axes and lifelines in their belts until the 1970s.

Qualified nurses were an exception to the general rule. The buckle was the only part of their uniform which was left entirely to their own choice. Although each teaching hospital had its own style of uniform, a tradition grew up that the buckle should be silver or silver plate, in the style of a clasp, and presented as a gift on passing the final exams or attaining the position of ward

Boys' Brigade buckle, as used between 1885 and 1926. Shown open and closed.

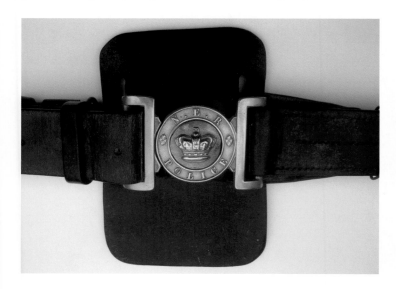

North Eastern Railway Police belt buckle. Victorian.

sister. It has been suggested that the clasp form was preferred as it left no belt ends or buckle prongs to get in the way. Silver was used because, as well as having a most attractive appearance, it was strong and could be safely sterilised.

HARNESS AND LUGGAGE

From Roman times and before, a buckle has been the only means by which straps and belts could be joined and quickly parted again. Their uses range far wider than merely as parts of clothing. From the time humans started to use horses or oxen they needed to be able to secure and release bridles and harnesses of all kinds. Sturdy buckles were an absolute necessity.

The industrial revolution of the eighteenth and nineteenth centuries and the centralisation of the manufacture of goods created a need for the

Horse-harness buckle from British Rail. Used 1948 onwards.

transportation of raw materials and the distribution of the finished product. Horses, already a vital part of agriculture, came into towns in great numbers to fulfil these tasks. The introduction of the railway system, largely replacing canals, brought a quicker method of moving goods and people but the expanding population and manufacturing capabilities generated an even greater need for horse transport. It has been reported that in the 1890s there were at least 25,000 horses in the carting trade alone in London. That indicates the need for a huge number of buckles.

The large railway companies had their initials on the buckles used on their own horses' harnesses, indicating the importance attached to the animals as part of the company network, and discouraging theft of the harness.

The introduction of the motor vehicle brought about a great change and a consequent reduction in the harness-buckle-making section of the industry. Many other uses of buckles have passed into history. Suitcases, bags and the school satchels carried by every child were all fastened with straps and buckles. Twenty-first-century luggage, often made of synthetic material, is usually fastened with zips or Velcro.

Horse-harness buckle from the Glasgow & South Western Railway, 1850 to 1923.

Brass buckle showing the attached thick leather. Steel prong.

MATERIALS

B Y the very nature of the demands put on them when in use, buckles have to be made of strong material. Through the years each change in fashion and each improvement in manufacturing techniques have increased the range of materials used in buckle-making.

METALS

Brass, an alloy of copper and zinc, has been used in buckle-making for hundreds of years. Consequently it is most difficult to date such buckles with any accuracy.

In the eighteenth century, when the various parts of buckles were made by different manufacturers, brass buckles frequently had iron bars, chapes and prongs. The chapes sometimes had spikes but this alone is not an indicator of age as the style continued into the twentieth century.

Early in the eighteenth century a clockmaker named Christopher Pinchbeck produced a variant on the alloy of copper and zinc which very closely resembled gold. This material, named after its inventor, was used in buckle-making. Gold was also used but the only real gold buckles which you may find are the very tiny ones from ladies' watchstraps.

Silver was an ideal material for buckle-making, being strong and durable but having a lovely glowing sheen. Any silver buckle may have a hallmark giving the date of manufacture, perhaps also the town where it was assayed and the maker. Unfortunately some eighteenth-century pieces are not fully marked. If you have a buckle in white metal of exactly the same design as one in silver it may be fair to use the silver example as a date indicator but this can be only conjecture.

White metal, the general term for any bright metallic compound, has been widely used for all styles of buckles. If it contains a proportion of iron, rust will form on it if it is allowed to remain in damp conditions.

Many metal buckles have marks on the back indicating that they were made in Czechoslovakia. The Czechoslovakian state was created in 1918 by the amalgamation of Bohemia, Moravia and Slovakia. The country exported

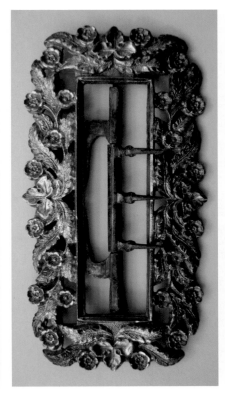

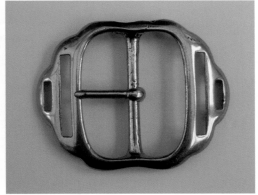

vast quantities of metal buckles to Britain, to the detriment of the industry in Birmingham, which had been the centre of British buckle-making.

To achieve permanent decorative effects on metal involves intricate processes. Since the advent of the general use of buckles in the fifteenth century, frames of malleable metal have been moulded into whatever style fashion demanded. When much handwork was involved in making buckles, designs were punched or engraved on the surface of the frames. With the invention of appropriate machinery, designs could be stamped using cut dies. Paints of all kinds can be used but are very easily chipped and damaged.

Manufacturers have always tried to produce an expensive-looking item in the cheapest possible manner so as to generate the greatest profit. To this end, silver plating was used to resemble solid silver. A particular process in which silver was fused on to a base metal, today referred to as Sheffield plate, was used for shoe buckles in the late eighteenth century. Electroplating was used in the nineteenth century. Tin plating also created a shiny finish. When used on a base of iron, it prevented the iron rusting but only while the surface

Above left: Buckle. Gilding on to copper. From the mid-nineteenth century.

Above right top: Small, ¾ inch, delicate buckle most likely used on a lady's watchstrap. Silver, London 1921.

Above right bottom: Buckle. Classic design in white metal. The registration number on the back dates it to 10 August 1905.

33

Buckles. The left one
is plated but closely
resembles the one on
right, which is silver,
Birmingham 1900.

Silver clasps and buckles. *Top* Revival art
nouveau clasp, Birmingham 1988.
Middle left Buckle, Chester 1894. *Middle right*
Buckle, Birmingham 1897. Both buckles are in
the rococo style. *Bottom* Clasp, Birmingham
1897.

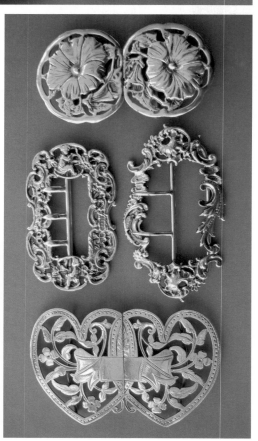

Shoe buckle. Eighteenth century. Sheffield plate.

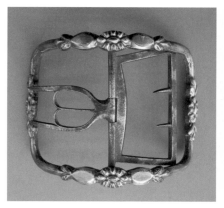

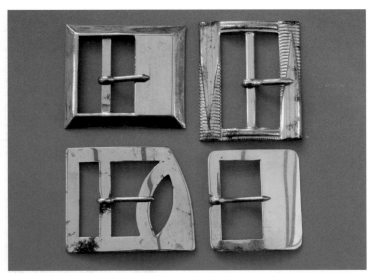

Selection of buckles c. 1930 with art deco influence, made from plated metal showing common forms of deterioration.

Clasp. Mirror glass mounted in brass. Marked 'Czechoslovakia Ges Gesch 81'.

Clasp. Pressed metal. Marked 'Czecho-slovakia'.

Slides. Cut steel. The large shoe slides, front and reverse, show individually set steel rivets. The small slides are made from one piece of metal pressed and cut to the required shape.

Shoe slides. *Top pair* Cut steel, individually polished and set. *Bottom, left and right* The frame has been plated, and moulded to the shape required. *Bottom, middle* Steel, cut and pressed to the shape required. All three pairs are leather backed and date from the late nineteenth/early twentieth century.

remained undamaged. Any scratch allowing damp to penetrate into the iron generated rusting on the surface.

Ornamentation added to the frame of a buckle in the form of polished rivets, effectively mimicking marcasites, was in vogue from the eighteenth century. It is known as 'cut steel'. The rivet heads of hardened steel were individually polished and set into the frame. The appearance was copied by moulding a pattern resembling rivet heads round the edge of the frame of the buckle. Cut steel can be seen on shoe buckles of the eighteenth century and shoe trims of the nineteenth and early twentieth centuries.

Diamanté decoration is an eternal favourite. In the eighteenth century, by candlelight, diamanté buckles must have looked most attractive. Diamanté may be called 'paste', 'brilliants', 'strass' or 'rhinestones' but essentially it is pieces of glass, perhaps with foil backing, set into a framework, and aiming to resemble diamonds. The durability of the item depends on this framework.

Cabochon settings, in which the glass is put into a cup of metal, the edges of which are bent over, is the most secure method for buckles. The prongs of claw settings are in danger of being snagged and bent, so loosening the pieces of glass. In the twentieth century there was a great demand for the cheap and cheerful, which prompted the mass production of poor-quality items. Diamanté decoration was made by gluing the glass pieces into indentations stamped into a shaped frame. However carefully you keep these examples, the glue can dry and the stones fall out.

Buckles. Diamanté. *Left* Claw setting. *Middle* Multiple claw setting. *Right* Large stones, cabochon setting; the rest are glued. Late nineteenth/early twentieth century.

Clasps. Diamanté. *Top* A mix of claw, cabochon and glued settings. *Bottom left* Glued setting. *Bottom right* Claw setting. All late nineteenth/early twentieth century.

Deco diamanté
clasp and buckle,
c. 1930s.

Shoe slides.
Diamanté. *Top left*
Marked 'France'.
Top right
Unmarked
coloured diamenté
Top *Middle row. Left
and right*
Composition,
marked 'Made in
France. Bte
SGDG'. *Centre pair*
Stones pavé set
into silver with
satin backing, from
the late eighteenth
century. *Bottom row*
Both pairs show
art nouveau
influence in design.
All, except the
middle pair, are
from the
nineteenth and
early twentieth
centuries.

A twenty-first
century buckle
with diamanté,
showing its return
to high fashion.

Adding colour to metal buckles cannot be satisfactorily accomplished by simply painting the surface. The imitation of enamelled styles using unfired paint is known as cold enamel. The way in which buckles are worn inevitably leads to damage. Enamelling, a more complicated and skilled process, offers a hard finish which will stand much more wear. Enamel paints, in the form of powdered glass, are fused to a metal base frame by firing. The frame must be rigid as, should it bend, the enamel will break away.

There are four types of enamelling which have been used in buckle-making. Probably the most common is champlevé in which the base-plate is stamped with indentations making up the design. The enamel is put into these wells for firing. If the enamelled buckle incorporated a suitably sized plain surface, hand-painted decoration could be added. In cloisonné enamelling indentations are created on the base by soldering on thin wires to create a picture or pattern. When different colours are added to each walled section

Clasps and slide. The centre slide, in champlevé enamelling, measures 4¾ inches from top to bottom. The clasps are of a mix of enamelling techniques with art nouveau influence to the designs. All from the nineteenth and early twentieth centuries.

Cloisonné enamel buckle. From the mid-nineteenth century.

Buckles. *Left and right* Both are from the second half of the nineteenth century and have deep champlevé wells, the surface having been painted with flowers. *Centre* Silver, Birmingham 1911, basse taille enamelling with a design of flowers and leaves cut into the base of the enamel well.

the total effect emerges. This technique involves both skill and time and cloisonné buckles are rare. Champlevé can be used to simulate a cloisonné appearance.

Enamel adheres to the base metal more securely if this metal surface is roughened. In the third and fourth types of enamelling, advantage is taken of this characteristic by adding clear or translucent enamel to a patterned plate. If an image or angular design has been hand-engraved or stamped into the base, the buckle may be described as 'basse taille', meaning base cut. If the base metal has an engine-turned or stamped linear design resembling intertwining ribbons, it may be called 'guilloche'.

Guilloche enamel slides and buckles. *Top, left and right pair* Silver, Birmingham 1910. *Top, centre* Silver, Birmingham 1909, with added flower decoration. *Bottom, left* Brass. *Bottom, centre* Clasp and slide, brass, c. 1930s deco. *Bottom, right* Silver, Birmingham 1911.

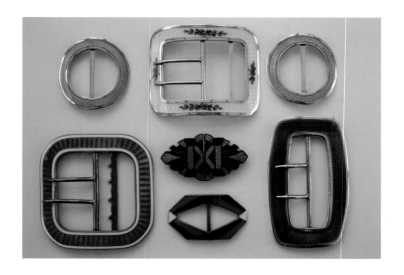

PEARL

Many lovely pearl buckles for ladies' dresses have been made from pearly shells. Because of the size of flat surface needed to make a buckle, oyster was most commonly used.

The quality and colour of pearl buckles vary. Layers of white and yellow through to brown or grey can be found. The pink or green mollusc shells usually only provide enough surface to make small trims or buckles. It is impossible, however, to ascertain the precise origin of the shell used in a buckle unless there is some outer layer remaining.

Under bright twenty-first-century lights pearl shell appears simply as a white or off-white but under the flickering half-light of candles or gas-lamps it gives off the most magnificent rainbow of colour.

The enduring popularity of pearl can be appreciated by the care taken to repair old pearl buckles. Even damaged prongs may be smoothed and rounded off so that the buckle can remain in use.

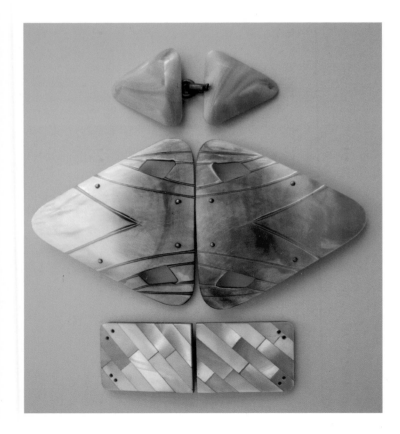

Pearl clasps. From the late nineteenth/early twentieth century.

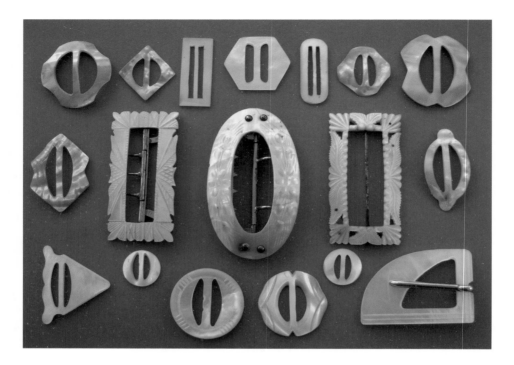

Above:
Pearl buckles and slides. The centre three are from the nineteenth century and have carved decoration. The remainder are from the late nineteenth/early twentieth century.

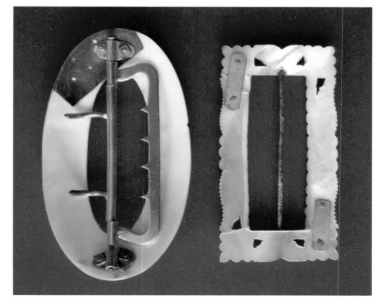

Right:
Reverse of the oval pearl buckle and the slide from the centre of the above picture showing intricate repair work.

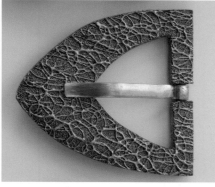

Wooden buckle and clasps. *Top left* Pressed and painted. *Bottom left* Stained and polished, marked 'Made in Czecho-slovakia. Registered'. *Right* The wood is decorated with barbola-type plasterwork and painted. All from the twentieth century.

WOOD

In times of hardship such as the depression of the 1930s or the two world wars, raw materials such as metals and some compositions, already in short supply, are vitally needed by industry. Buckles become a very low priority. Makers turn to wood as a material to produce a cheap article.

There were attempts made to brighten the dull appearance with painted designs or plasterwork embellishments. However, if these buckles were ever washed, the decoration came off immediately. Many wooden buckles were

Original card with a buckle and matching buttons made from pressed and painted wood, *c.* 1930s.

43

made with an impressed design, some of which show the art deco influence in offset patterns and shapes.

Wood, being easily worked by hand or with simple machinery, was most suitable for use by studio craftspeople, and individually made examples can be found.

LEATHER

Although a frame and bar of leather would alone not be substantial enough to carry a prong, leather has been used to cover cheap materials to create an attractive buckle.

Suede dyed to tone with a lady's garment was widely used in the 1930s. The belted gabardine mackintosh worn by men after the Second World War had a slim, rectangular, leather-covered buckle. This style of buckle was so entrenched that exact replicas were later made for mackintoshes in moulded plastic and metal.

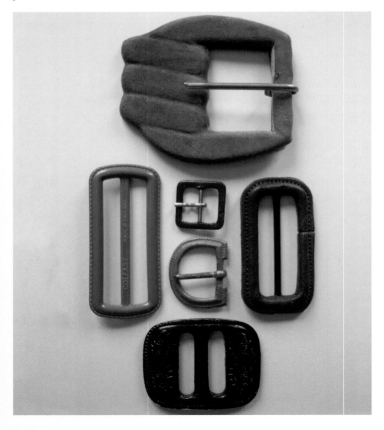

Leather. *Top* Buckle, thick cardboard covered in dyed suede. *Middle row, left and right* Slides of the type used on the belts of gabardine mackintoshes in the middle of the twentieth century; the right one is metal covered with leather, the left one an imitation of that style of composition, marked 'Colfast – made in England'. *Middle row, upper centre* Buckle, leather over metal. *Middle row, lower centre* Buckle, metal moulded to resemble leather. *Bottom* Pressed leather slide.

GLASS

It is not surprising that very few buckles made entirely of glass have survived. Glass was used mainly as a means of decorating metal buckles.

After Prince Albert died in 1861 black became the colour generally worn in Britain. Black glass beads, buttons, dress decorations and buckles were in demand.

Some ingenuity was needed to make a strong, lightweight, black glass buckle which blended with the dress adornments. One method employed was the gluing of individual discs of glass to a metal frame of the required shape. Another method, which was much more fragile, was to set a wire into the back of a glass disc. The wire holding the disc was then threaded through a hole in the fretted frame of the buckle. The protruding end on the back was either bent over to secure it or treated like a rivet and splayed out. The back was then covered with a thick layer of japanning. These buckles, with so many sharp edges and spikes to catch on cloth, must have been difficult to wear.

Mirrored glass, giving a sparkling reflection, was used to decorate some buckles. Coloured glass made to imitate various hardstones gave buckles a

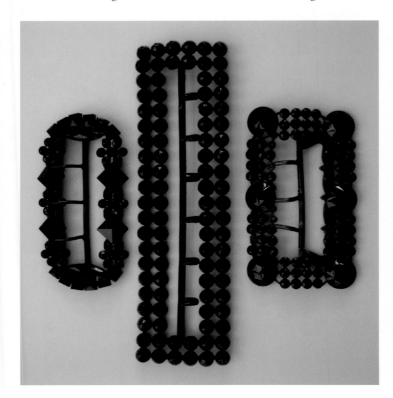

Buckles. Black glass. The centre buckle measures 5½ inches. All are from the mid to late nineteenth century.

Buckle, slides and clasp. Glass or with glass decorations. *Top, middle* Painted reverse moulding, marked 'Czecho Slovakia'. All from the first half of the twentieth century.

Left:
Black glass. The reverse of the buckle at the right-hand side of the picture on page 45, showing its construction.

Right:
Clasps. Glass of deco design, *c.* 1930s. *Top and middle* Marked 'Czechoslovakia'.

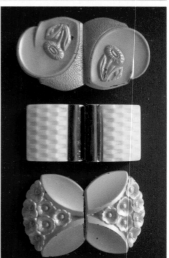

Clasp. Plaques of millefiori glass mounted on white metal. From the twentieth century.

touch of splendour. Reverse mouldings into glass frames were painted, the foremost section being painted first and the background last. This created a wonderful three-dimensional effect but the paint was easily damaged if the buckle was washed.

In the first half of the twentieth century glass clasps were highly fashionable. Imports from Czechoslovakia fulfilled this demand, many with striking art deco designs. Sadly, probably due to the vulnerability of the material, you frequently find just one half of the clasp.

COMPOSITIONS

In the twentieth century, plastic compounds began to be used for buckles. Celluloid, although invented in 1869, was used sparingly as decoration until it was produced on a wider commercial scale after the First World War. Casein, Bakelite and a wide variety of other plastics were also in use. After the Second World War there was a great expansion in the chemical industries and from then on such materials formed the basis of the buckle-making industry.

Buckles and slides in various plastic compounds. *Middle, right* Marked 'Made in England'. All from the early twentieth century.

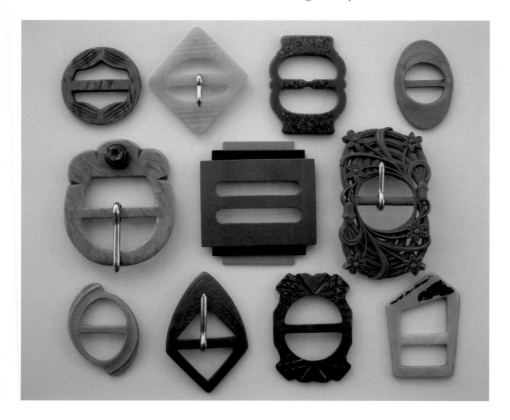

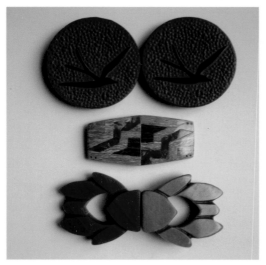

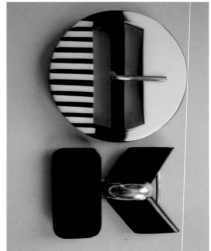

Above left: Clasps in various plastic compounds. The middle one is marked 'Bte SGDG'. All from the early twentieth century.

Above right: Deco-design clasp and buckle.

Right: Clasps, slides and a buckle. All celluloid covering over metal, c. 1930s with deco designs.

During the first half of the twentieth century the home dress-making market generated a considerable demand for buckles. The deprivations of the times forced many women to make their own and their children's clothes. Plastic buckles that were cheap, washable and easy to use by the needlewomen were in demand. Under the wartime rationing schemes introduced from June 1941 buckles were categorised as 'hard haberdashery' and were, as such, exempt from coupons.

In the 1960s and 1970s inflation and other market forces brought an increase in the price of cloth and needlework items. This, coupled with the availability of cheap imported clothes, largely brought an end to home dress-making. In the last years of the twentieth century, dress for both men and women changed to a more loose-fitting style with less use of belt and buckles.

EXOTIC BUCKLES

A high-quality intricately made buckle, like a piece of jewellery, can look good on any woman's dress. When fashion included a belted waist, buckles were in demand and any very special example was a most appreciated gift.

In the Far East highly skilled carvers, jewellery workers and enamellers could create fantastic buckles, and with the cheap labour costs in those parts these pieces would sell within a reasonable price range for the European market.

Between the mid-nineteenth and early twentieth centuries, Japan was eager to earn European currency to enable the purchase of technically advanced goods. Export of their artwork helped them to achieve their aim. Although Japanese women still wore traditional dress, fastenings suitable for European fashion became part of these sales.

Hand-painted Satsuma porcelain discs, the pottery named from the province of Japan where it was made, were mounted in metal to make clasps. The detail of the painting is exquisite. Enamellers, also, included clasps amongst their products, the designs, although essentially Japanese, contributed to the inspiration of the art nouveau style.

Clasp. Satsuma plaques mounted in metal, from the nineteenth or early twentieth century.

Clasp. Turquoise tesserae showing much hand-work. Of Middle Eastern origin.

Left: Buckle. Carved ivory set on to gilt metal, from the mid-nineteenth century.

Right: Clasps. *Top* South Asian moulded silver. The clasp closes with a slot-and-slide construction. *Middle* Russian niello-work on silver with the Cyrillic lettering 'KAVKAS' meaning Caucasus. The silver marks date to 1896–1908. *Bottom* West African silver.

Clasp. Enamel on
copper. Plain dark
green enamel on
reverse of clasp.
Japanese. From the
nineteenth or early
twentieth century.

Middle Eastern craftsmen specialising in metalwork produced unusual buckles for the English market. These appealed to devotees of the aesthetic movement of the late nineteenth century. The jewellers made many objects from turquoise tesserae work including buckles.

As travel and tourism increased and widened in the twentieth century so did the range of imported goods and souvenirs brought back by travellers. Buckles of this era made from coconut shell can be found, the design indicating their country of origin. West African craftsmen usually worked on beaten brass but high-quality silver was more suitable for the overseas market.

Clasp. The Chinese
characters for
'good luck' and
'long life'. These
are the traditional
greetings at the
Chinese New Year
and have become a
classic design.

COLLECTING AND DISPLAY

Hɪsᴛᴏʀʏ has a habit of repeating itself and, as two hundred years ago, buckles have again become a status symbol. However, it is body-style not wealth that is being flaunted today. As a result of the twenty-first century's obsession with healthy eating and weight, anyone with a waist size of which they are proud wants to accentuate it with a belt and buckle.

There is an abundance of well-made buckles to choose from, many of which will be the collectables of the future. Fashion houses are using the trend to promote themselves by featuring their logo in their designs. Some manufacturers are making buckles to an individual's own requirements, such items destined to become a most treasured possession. Film companies have specifically designed buckles to sell to film fans as memorabilia.

On the rodeo circuit in America, buckles for use on jeans, depicting bulls and cowboys, were given as prizes. The same style of heavy metal buckle has been produced for the British market in a great variety of designs. Many of these have been made in numbered limited editions to add exclusivity and create the foundations for a collectors' market.

Collecting buckles is a fascinating and worthwhile hobby. It leads you into discovering more about both social history and manufacturing

Spider Man buckle and belt. From the twenty-first century.

Above left: Buckle. Diamanté. A prong on the reverse of the frame fixes into the weave of the lattice-work belt. From the twenty-first century.

Above right: Patriotic buckle. Produced during the 1930s for the Jubilee and the Coronation. (*Courtesy of The Holley/Cornelius Collection, Bletchley Park*)

techniques and materials. Buckles can be bought from antique shops or craft and 'boot' fairs at a wide variety of prices. They are easy to display, mounted on belts or strips of ribbon, making a most attractive wall feature for any room. Perhaps the most appealing aspect of buckle-collecting is that you can wear the buckles yourself.

Below:
Selection of clasps. The one in the centre is Satsuma ware; the remainder are enamel. All from the nineteenth and early twentieth centuries.

Jeans buckles. *Left to right. Top* Snake with red enamel. 'MAG', Motorbike Action Group, commemorating its twenty-fifth anniversary. Stonehenge souvenir. *Bottom* Stonehenge souvenir. St George and the Dragon in enamel-work. Biker's buckle. All from the late twentieth and into the twenty-first century.

Below: *Left* An Excelsior composition buckle on its original card. Priced at 1s. 9d (9p). From the mid-twentieth century. *Middle* A lady's dress buckle on its original card, *c.* 1930s. *Right* A DIY buckle on its original card. Priced at 1s. 7d (8p). From the mid-twentieth century.

IDENTIFICATION OF BACK MARKS

Breveté French. Patented
Déposé French. Registered
Geschutzt German. Protected
Gesellschaft German. Society or company
SGDG (Sans Garantie du Gouvernement) French. Without government guarantee

FURTHER READING

BOOKS ON BUCKLES
Cuddeford, M. J. *Identifying Buckles*. Mount Publications, 1996.
Hawthorne, Ran. *Railway Horse Brasses*. National Horse Brass Society, 1987.
Swann, June. *Shoe Buckles: Catalogue*. Northampton Museum, 1981.

BACKGROUND INFORMATION
Cunnington, Phillis, and Lucas, Catherine. *Occupational Costume in England*. A & C Black,
    London, 1967.
De Marly, Diana. *Fashion for Men*. Batsford, London, 1985.
Page, C. *Foundations of Fashion*. Leicestershire Museums, 1981.
Swann, June. *Shoemaking*. Shire Publications, Princes Risborough/
    Oxford, 2003.
Wilson, E., and Taylor, L. *Through the Looking Glass*. BBC Books,
    London, 1989.

INDEX

Page numbers in italic refer to illustrations